Camp

Bess Wohl made her Broadway debut in 2019 with her play
Grand Horizons, for which she received a Tony Award
nomination. Other theatre includes: *Small Mouth Sounds* –
OCC Award, *Make Believe* – OCC Award, *Continuity*,
American Hero, *Barcelona*, *Touched*, *In*, *Cats Talk Back* and
Pretty Filthy. Her plays have been produced at theatres in
NY, around the US and internationally. Awards include the
Sam Norkin Special Drama Desk Award, the Georgia Engel
Playwriting Award, a MacDowell Fellowship and inclusion
on Hollywood's Black List of Best Screenplays. Wohl is an
Associate Artist with The Civilians, an alumna of Ars Nova's
Play Group, and holds new play commissions from
Manhattan Theatre Club and Williamstown. She has also
written for film/television, and is a graduate of Harvard and
the Yale School of Drama.

BESS WOHL

Camp Siegfried

faber

First published in 2021
by Faber and Faber Limited
74–77 Great Russell Street
London WC1B 3DA

Typeset by Brighton Gray
Printed and bound in the UK by CPI Group (Ltd), Croydon CR0 4YY

A CIP record for this book
is available from the British Library

978-0-571-37487-8

2 4 6 8 10 9 7 5 3 1

Camp Siegfried was first performed at The Old Vic, London, on 7 September 2021, with the following cast and creative team:

Her Patsy Ferran
Him Luke Thallon

Understudies
Her Lauren Koster
Him Ed McVey

Director Katy Rudd
Set and Costume Rosanna Vize
Lighting Prema Mehta
Sound Ian Dickinson for Autograph
Video Tal Rosner
Movement Rachel-Leah Hosker
Casting Jessica Ronane CDG
Voice Charlie Hughes-D'Aeth
Dialect Rebecca Gausnell
Associate Set and Costume Anisha Fields
Baylis Assistant Director Jasmine Teo

Stage Management Maria Gibbons, Daniel Roach-Williams, Tamsin Withers

Characters

Him
Her

CAMP SIEGFRIED

Note

The play takes place in the summer of 1938
at Camp Siegfried.

Camp Siegfried was a German-American summer camp
located in Yaphank on Long Island.

It operated from 1936 to 1941.

/ denotes where the next character should begin speaking.

His dialogue is in italics.

Hers is in standard type.

SCENE ONE

A festive, German-style dance hall.

Lit by bulbous strands of outdoor lights.

A German oompah band plays.
    Ooom pah pah, ooom pah pah.

Very loud.

She is standing alone.
    Drinking a beer.

She's not used to drinking beer.
    She's sixteen.
    She winces at the taste.

He comes over.
    He speaks first.

Or shouts, really.
    An indecipherable salutation.
    He's seventeen.

They are both golden.
    She is pale.
    He is more of a rose.

Most of this scene should be shouted.
    It's okay if we miss some of it.

There's punch

What

If you don't like the beer there's

Oh
It's okay
Someone just handed this to me
It's okay

Pause.

Having fun?

Me

Who else

Oh!
Yeah sure I guess
Sure

You look a little glum

What

Glum
GLUM
GLUM!

Oh
No / I'm fine

Cheer up

Oh
What

Cheer up
It's camp

Right

You gotta have fun

Right
What
Sorry it's just the music it's so

Wanna dance

Me

Who else dummy

Oh no
No no no no no no no
I'm a terrible dancer
No no no no no no no

I don't buy that for a

No I am
Oh trust me
Oh gosh I just

     She laughs convulsively.

What

Just thinking about it
No no no no no no no

     Her laughing almost seems painful.
       He watches her.

First summer here

I know!

What?

Sorry what was the question

Is it your first summer at camp

Oh
Yes!
Yours?

We come out every year from New York
Well past two years anyway since the place started
My grandparents bought one of the bungalows actually
I'll mostly be in the tents

My parents too

They're in the bungalows?

No
No no no
What I mean is
They live in Baltimore

Baltimore

Is that interesting?

(*Laughs.*) *No!*

I'm sorry I think
Ohhhh
I think I got too much sun today at the lake

It's okay

Too much beer maybe
Maybe I should stop drinking this

No you're fine
You were saying
Baltimore

Yes!
But they sent me up here because
My aunt
She has one of the bungalows

Your

AUNT
And so she keeps telling me to come out
She keeps inviting me every summer
Come to camp
Come to camp
Blah blah blah blah camp

So you're living with her

So this year my parents were like you have to go
Blah blah blah

Well sure it's about time
'Carpe Diem'

I love Latin!
Anyway my aunt thinks I need to get more physical exercise
Move around more
Be in the sun the fresh air

Sure

Things fester in dark spaces
That's what she says
And I think by dark spaces she just means Baltimore
She's over there somewhere with the
With the clogs and the kind of a face like a horse

That one?

No!
With the pigtails
Well I guess they all have pigtails
Wait now she just went behind
The the the tuba player
That's her
The pigtails
With the green the green bows

Ohhhh
With the accordion

> *She awkwardly mimes playing the accordion.*

Oh!

She plays that thing all day long
She sings too
Tippy-top of her lungs
Even Pickles hides under the sofa when he hears her start
up
That's the cat

> *He laughs.*

7

Well don't worry
You'll love it here
There's all kinds of swimming and sports

Oh no no no
I'm no good at sports
I'm scared of swimming
I'm terrified of the ocean

You can hike right

I don't know

If you can walk you can hike
One foot in front of the other

I guess

There's cook-outs sing-a-longs movie-nights dances
Ghost stories survival skills
Contests like spear throwing and shot put and you can win
prizes
And one of the boys
The best one who wins the most contests and stuff
At the end of the summer he
Even gets to be youth leader and the youth leader picks the
Youth speaker at German Day

What is

What is German Day?!
It's a huge celebration
Thousands of people swarm up here

Oh gosh I hate crowds

(Laughs.) Okay okay
How 'bout sailing

Oh no no no no no

Why not?

I'm always scared of the thing
The thing that
Comes across the

The boom

Yes

Oh come on dummy
You don't need to be scared of that
You just duck

> *Pause.*

Why are you even

I try to meet the new people
Meet the new people

Ohhhhh
I understand
I need to stop drinking this beer
It's making me woooooozy
(*Re: the band.*) Oh no they're coming closer

I love this song

> *She cracks up.*

I do
See you can't even embarrass yourself in front of me
I think I'm gonna dance
Come on it's fun

Okay yeah
Okay go dance
I'll no no no no
Be here so

> *He starts to go, but.*

Hey
Where are you staying?

9

Yeah you
Where are you staying with
Your aunt?

Oh
On Hitler
Hitler Way
You?

We're corner of Hitler and Goebbels

The white one?

Yeah

With the yellow

Yeah

That's just

Right there
Yeah
So
Must be fate

> *The band, the band, the band.*

> *End of scene.*

Outside.
  Fresh air.
  He is chopping wood.
  With an axe.

She is bringing him logs.

They are in German camp outfits.
  He's mid-history lesson.

*. . . So basically my great-grandpa had a dairy farm back in
Germany with cows you know and the whole thing and
they worked the land back then hard honest work he's just
farming the land then one day my grandpa he's working the
farm not much older than me and sees in the papers there's
gold in California endless fields of wheat in Nebraska!
America! You know land of opportunity*

Sure

*So he takes off he's going west but of course he gets here
Meets my grandma never gets past New York
That's a whole romantic story
Anyway he opens a furniture store first on Delancey then up
In Yorkville do you know Yorkville
That's uptown where all the Germans are*

Uh-huh

*My dad grows up starts making furniture for it
German stuff quality stuff
But then with the Depression and all you know when that
hit*

My dad started doing carpentry fix-it-up kinda jobs
He likes it
It's pretty good
Nobody's doing much home renovations these days
But still things break

Sure

Sometimes he still builds a piece of furniture here and there
Like he built a porch swing that was
Well it ended up being
A foot too big for our porch

Oh no

Yeah I think he'd been drinking though
Anyway
I'm itching to go out west when I get the chance
Wanna fulfil my grandpa's dream
Maybe make it to Nebraska

Wow

There's lots of us out there
Germans I mean
But I mean
How much do you even know about German history actual
real German history and facts

Not a lot
I guess

> *Pause.*
> > *He continues to chop.*

You know we invented Kindergarten

You invented

I mean Germans
'Kinder' means kid obviously

Right obviously
What did you invent exactly

Not me dummy
/ Germans

No I mean what did they invent exactly
It's just a place to drop off your kid

It's Kindergarten

It's just school but for five-year-olds

Yeah
It's school but for five-year-olds

Okay

> *Pause.*
> > *He chops more wood.*

Also Christmas

That is not

That is
Sure
That's German
That's a hundred per cent from Germany
Santa Claus
He's German
Mistletoe

Right
I knew / that

Also
We've got

Oktoberfest

> *Chop.*

Beer

Chop.

Hamburgers
Hot dogs

Oh gosh the hot dogs here

I know

I have to stop eating them
They're so – big

Okay

No I mean in one week I think
I've had about fifty of them that's all

I know

What

People are talking about it

What!?!

No come on dummy you're perfect
I'm German on both sides
You?

Oh well I
My mom is
My dad might have some English or something

Don't apologise for it

The English or something

Being German
You look all hangdog about it
'My mom is . . .'

Well you know how sauerkraut's
Liberty cabbage now and hamburgers are liberty sandwiches
And we're all Barbarians and Huns and everything

Don't listen to that

I know but the kids at my school

They call you that?

You've never been called a Hun

I'd take it as a point of pride

Really?

Sure, why not?
Raaargh,
I'm a Hun
Ich bin ein fürchterlicher Hunne
Run for your lives!
Rennt um euer Leben –

You're the scary Hun who invented Kindergarten!
And Santa Claus!

I'm a scary Christmas Hun!

Anyway, I guess it's different for a girl

Why?

I don't know, 'barbarian' . . .

What?

It sounds like hairy legs
So anyway I don't advertise about it honestly
My mom won't even speak German
I barely even speak a word

You / don't

Just my dad when he's angry
My mom says
I don't know
She says people will think that we put babies on spikes

Who'll think that?
The Irish? The Italians?
The Jews?

Oh no
I don't know
I mean I don't even know any Jews

You've seen 'em in picture books though

I guess

> *Pause.*

You don't get tired do you?!

I'd rather this than trash duty

Oh I know

Or toilets

But isn't it
You know shouldn't there be
It seems unfair that the what do you call it the Youth

The Jugendschaft

Right yeah it seems unfair that we have to do everything

What do you mean

Just the cleaning and building and electrical wiring

Well what else do you expect dummy
We can't hire a bunch of outsiders can we

Well no I mean I don't know
Why not

Spies dummy

What

Every year there's some hack
Some government guy

Oh
Really?

Posing as 'German' tries to come up here and catch us

Catch us at what

Who knows?
Having fun?
But
There's always some some
Some hack some whiny little guy like 'Dickstein'

Who is Dickstein

You know they tried
They tried to take this place away from us
The whole town of Yaphank
They tried to stop us
They said our bugles were

The bugles are loud
And they start very early in the
Sorry go on

And my dad said only thing that stopped 'em was when we
said
Fine all right we'll sell the land sure fine
How 'bout we sell to the Negroes

Oh that's

That sure stopped 'em dead in their tracks
All of a sudden they're all sure you keep it you're fine
You German folk can stick around
My dad's like oh so by 'American values' you meant
'Property' values

(*Laughs.*) Oh that's terrible

Bunch of hypocritical pencil-pushing anti-American
Half of 'em are in the KKK

And they come after us
Last summer they flew over dumping leaflets

Saying what?

I don't know
They think we've all pledged allegiance to Hitler

Have you

Aw come on
Herr Kuhn sent him a telegram
He never even responded
I mean come on
We're Americans
My dad fought in the war
That's the American flag flying up there
Wait
(Playing.) You're not a spy are you

Me
A spy
Oh no I'm
Wait
How do I know you're not the spy

> *She stares at him.*
> > *Pause.*

How 'bout some more wood

What?

More wood
Whoever chops the most gets a badge
Whoever gets the most badges gets 'Youth Leader'
Whoever gets 'Youth Leader' picks 'Youth Speaker'

And what's it all for

The

The wood

The bonfire dummy
It's so huge they say you can see the smoke all the way
To Islip
We're going to
Roast Things

Oh
Fun!

Gotta win / this one

Yes fun okay!

> *She runs off.*

(*From off.*) OW!

(*Calls.*) *You okay?*

(*From off.*) Yeah I'm fine
I'm fine I'm fine I'm fine

> *She comes back*
> *Carrying way, way too many logs.*

Whoa okay whoa
Take it easy pigtails

No I got this
I do I can

Here let me
Whoa what are you trying to / kill yourself or something

Owww sorry

Careful
Here let me take that
It's okay

I'm sorry
I'm hopeless

We got to toughen you up / pigtails

I'm sorry
I'm a klutz really

You okay?

I think I just
I got a splinter

> *He looks at her.*
> > *Suddenly she's in tears.*

Hey
Hey hey hey

No it's not that I'm just
It's fine
It's just that I hate myself

> *He takes her hand.*

Hey
It's okay
Let me

No
You don't have to

It's in pretty deep
Let me just

> *He tries to squeeze her fingers.*

Ouch ow ow ow
Sorry
It just hurts

Hold on
Don't touch it
You don't want to break off the tip
It'll go further in
Just let me

He reaches in his pocket.
    Pulls out a Swiss Army knife.

Aaaaah
Don't cut it off!

Would you relax?
There's tweezers in here

    He looks at her for a moment.

Oh
Please be

    He pulls out the tweezers.

Hey
Hold still
Hold still I said
Trust me

    She closes her eyes.

I do

    He works on her finger.

    End of scene.

The bonfire crackles.
  They sit, staring out.

They may have meat on sticks.

The fire is hot and red.
  It flickers on their faces.

The sound of crackling.

Little embers fly into the air.

They are drinking.

She is looser now, laughing, drunk.

. . . So wait so wait so wait so wait so wait so wait
Long Island
Is not an island?

It's a peninsula really
It's a very long peninsula it's
Light on both sides that's what makes it so damn bright
/ All the time

So all right but then so that makes no sense
Why don't they call it
Long Peninsula

Ring-Ring all aboard the Siegfried Special
Train to 'Long Peninsula'

Why not?

Not to mention
Nobody'd ever know how to spell it on an envelope

Easy
P-E-N-I-S
Wait no oh gosh / oh gosh oh gosh

See what I mean

Anyway I don't even know if I believe you on all this anyway
About any of this I'm going to ask Fräulein Linda about all of this
Tomorrow before her lecture tomorrow

You go to those dumb lectures?!

She shows movies!

Ohhh but she's so boring blah blah blah
'Obligated to America tied to Germany
Me for you you for me Volksgemeinschaft Wagner
Blah blah Siegfried / blah blah blah'

He's the great dragon slayer
The 'one who does not know fear'

Oh come on he gets duped by the gods and then killed

And Brunhilde! Kriegreprincessen der Walkürn!
Ohh my German

You'll get there

Throwing herself on his funeral pyre!
Now that is love
Fearless love
Can you imagine
I'm scared of everything basically all the time

Come on

Oh no I am I told you

The ocean you said

Dogs bugs getting hit in the face with a baseball
Water cavities in my teeth wood picking up wood sitting on wood

Okay

My mom says I'm just a caterpillar
One day I'll be a butterfly
If I don't get stepped on first

She's a philosopher

She's a librarian

Ah

And so it makes no sense
How she's mad because I spend all my time
In the library studying Latin poetry
Which seems useless to her probably because it is useless
But anyway I guess the point is
What was I saying

Tell me a poem

What?
Tell you a poem?!

Shoot that came out dumb
/ I'm a blittle bit drunk

No
Well maybe yes me too
A blittle bit
I can't believe I ate all of that bratwurst
I basically want to kill myself

Well don't do that

Okay!
Well
You know 'Odi et amo'

No
I told you I don't know any of that Latin Poetry

Don't say it like that

Like what

'That Latin Poetry'

Fine
I don't know any

    Sudden, intense, fully embodied.

Odi et amo
I hate and I love
Why do I do it
I don't know
But I feel it
And I am burned alive

    Pause.
        He stares at her.
        She stares at the fire.

I requested you

You what
For what

Chores tomorrow
We're laying brick
We've got a whole stage to build

A stage
For what

A platform
With a coupla hedges cut up like the German flag on either
side

That sounds hard

Nah it's just like in Nuremberg

You mean Nuremberg Nuremberg

Just like on the newsreels / at the movies

Ohhhh

And it all has to be ready by German Day

It's for

And maybe even Hitler

What
You mean he might be / coming

It's just what I heard

To Yaphank
The real Hitler

For German Day maybe

But why

He likes what we're doing dummy
He's always been impressed with / how we handle things in
America

Wait so no wait
That's so that's so that's
Who we're
Building a stage for

That's the idea

But isn't he a little bit crazy

Nah that's just his style

He seems very excitable

Look at what he's done for Germany
He's turned everything around
My brother went over there
Met him
Well not met him but saw him
Back in the Olympics

Uh-huh

And you know Jesse Owens said he felt more respected in
Germany than here in America so

Hitler wouldn't even shake his hand

And you know the Olympic torch

Do I?

That was all Hitler's idea
Not the torch but the fact that they carried it

Who

The Olympians the athletes
They carried this torch all the way from Greece
And the flame never went out
All the way from Greece through Hungary Yugoslavia
Austria
All the way to Berlin
And it never went out
It's the light of of of
Freedom!

The light of progress!
The future!
Our bright future
That's what he wants for us
Are you in

I
I can't

What

I should have
I should have told you before
Or maybe I shouldn't I don't know
Oh gosh I just

What

There's a boy

Anyway it's all a big mess I mean
I mean
The number of times my aunt has told me
Don't make the mistakes your mother made
Don't marry an Italian

Wait what
Your dad's Italian

No
The boy
Just on his mother's side
His dad's I don't know what his dad is actually
And anyway

Is it serious

No
I don't know

That's why they sent you away to camp

Well and also I don't play any sports
And anyway I guess the point is
I'm not turning out the way anyone wants me to

Oh

I'm sorry

For what
Forget it
That's not what I was after anyway dummy come on

Right sure I didn't mean
Oh gosh I'm such a dummy

Anyway I'm gonna

Wait where
Don't leave
Where are you going

I'll be back I'll be back I think I just need ahhh
More beer

> *He stagger-runs off.*
>
> *She stares at the fire.*
>
> *End of scene.*

SCENE FOUR

They are laying brick for the base of the stage.

They are also drinking beer.

She's bent over obsessively smoothing caulk.

He's hauling wheelbarrows of bricks.

Uhhhhhhhgh it's not straight
No no no no no it's all wrong

Looks okay to me

No it's not straight it's not straight
You didn't put the line straight and so the bricks aren't right
and then by the time I get there the whole thing's gonna fall
over

It's 'cause you've got 'em touching the line

No they're not
Where

Right there right look

Because you said put the bricks right up next to the line

I said

Hair's breadth / from the line

I said next to the line not touching the line
You touch the line I told you this / it gets all outta whack

Well thank you yes

See that's gonna be all outta

Yes I can see that now
I see that thank you

Just nudge that guy in

No 'cause it won't be level now
Don't push it down don't push it down the
You're getting the
Get away get away get away from my bricks
I'll start over
It's fine

>   *Pause.*
>   *She furiously pulls apart some bricks.*

Why are you mad

I'm not mad

You seem mad

Why would I be mad

Okay

I'm tired I'm just tired
I was at that stupid bonfire last night
Till all hours

Right

And then I finally get to bed and then
Fräulein Evelyn called my stupid aunt at midnight
And had her wake me up for some horrible midnight hike
Which honestly why do they do that to us

It was a full moon

Well I'm glad you had fun
I didn't get back until practically dawn and
My legs are all scratched up and

Lemme see your legs

No way

Just pull down your socks
Don't be a dummy
You don't want to get 'em infected do you
Let me see

> *She carefully pulls down her socks.*
> *Her legs are smeared with blood.*

Oh yikes that's bad
Maybe you should see Krankenschwester Betsy

What is that

The camp nurse

I don't need the nurse
I'm fine

It looks bad

No forget it
I'm not some kind of a whaddyoucallit
Fräulein Hoffer called it a schneeballwefer

A what

A schneeballwefer you know
A person who throws / schneeballs

Snowballs

With gloves on
Fräulein Hoffer was talking about it in my German class
I'm the best one

Handschuhschneeballwerfer

Right a handschuhschneeballwerfer

Nice German

Ich bin eine harte Arbeiterin
I told you I've worked the hardest

Good yes
I can see that

And I can handle getting my hands cold
I'm fine
I don't need gloves

Well you oughta at least clean them off
Your legs

Don't touch my legs

    He takes out a handkerchief.

Don't touch me
Don't come any closer
Don't
Don't pretend that you
Care about
What happens to me

What
What are you

I saw you go last night
After you said you'd come back then I I I
I saw you run off
Into the woods
With
Katie Hoxberg

So what

So I saw that
The moonlight was bright I know it was

Okay
So what
You told me you had a boyfriend

So you immediately

What was I supposed to

The moment
The very night that I told you about

It's camp
We're supposed to be social

Well you and Katie looked very social
Also
Tommy Lange might ask me to the
Tanzparty this weekend so
But I'm hoping Mikey Albrecht will ask because
I think he's dreamy and he has the most badges anyway so
Who even cares

Fine

Fine

So what

So nothing

And anyway you did say that you had a boyfriend

I do
Trust me
He just wrote me
A very beautiful letter

> *She exhales angrily pulls back up her bloody socks and*
> *goes back to the brickwork.*
>
> *Then:*

Look
I'm trying to put this delicately

You think I'm ugly

What?
No where'd you get that information dummy

Oh sorry no you just said

I'm talking about Katie now
Gosh you're not you're you're

Never mind
What about her

The point is like I said
We're supposed to be social and

Stop saying 'social'

It's the whole point of being here
Well part of it anyway
It's part of the 'Kampf'

Stop saying kampf just say camp

No 'Kampf', it's the the the fight the struggle
It doesn't mean camp dummy
It's the struggle to

What

Okay so everyone here is pure German
Mostly at least

So

So they want us to socialise

Oh
Ohhhh you mean because

I mean
Did you ever wonder
The Jungen tents are only less than
Ten feet away from the Mädchen tents

I'm with my aunt in the

Okay but okay
Do you even have a curfew

No 'cause she's always out at the Biergarten

'Cause she wants you to be social
You should have seen it last night
The whole woods was full of Jungen and Mädchen
And by the end of the summer half those girls will be
expecting

Oh because

It's our duty as pure Germans you see
To
Make more of us

But isn't that a little bit strange
I mean 'pure Germans'

Well honestly
When you look at all the bad people in America
Like the Commies immigrating all the time
Right up to the government the FBI the people undermining
America
It's a pretty good idea
It's patriotic

Wait

What

So that's why no just that's why
She was squawking around at breakfast this morning

Who was

Katie

What was / she saying

Just bragging all about the two of you

Well it's nobody's beeswax

Exactly
But you know
She was nattering on about a million things

Like what

Everybody just wanted her to clam up
So we could eat our jelly donuts in peace
She talks a lot that one and her voice is so

What else did she say

I'm trying to remember exactly
Hmmmm
Well all the girls were nattering on about
One of them went in the woods with Johnny Ryan
And another with Malcolm Mueller and what's the one
The tall boy with the hideous freckles
And then Tillie Becker said it's
Ein Schande and Sie Haben Sex
And I understood it because my German is really coming
along   '
It's amazing
Fräulein Linda says I'm the best out of the girls and the
boys

Okay but Katie

Oh right so I was sitting just eating my donut
Jelly donut
And everyone's yammering and nattering on
And then Squawky pipes up to say that
She went in the woods with you
And she's hoping she might be you know
But then again

Then again

She doesn't think there's much of a chance

> *He looks wounded.*

You mean

Well it wasn't because of her
It was more what you
That you

She said that

Anyway girls can be mean

Well whatever she said it's not true

And it's none of my / beeswax anyway

It's not true I said
Christ –
It's her fault –
It's the beer
I'm always so fucking drunk –

Hey it's just stupid girls talking

You don't think I know that?

So fine so don't let it get to you

I'm not

I shouldn't have even said anything
It doesn't matter

Yeah right
Now everybody thinks I'm defective or something
Weak
Like my dad says I'm weak
No 'Kampfgeist'

Camp spirit?

No Kampfgeist I told you it's
I told you
Kampf is struggle
It's the fighter's spirit
The spirit of the fight

    Pause.
      He's in pain.

You have that

What do you know
You're a kid

I'm sixteen
How old are you

Seventeen

So

So that's a big difference

Yeah right
It's not that big of a difference
I know things
I know more than those dumb girls in the cafeteria

Yeah right

I've done it plenty

You have

Yeah and honestly
I mostly can't figure out
What the big deal is

You

I mean all of this stuff has been written about it
And said about it
And 'Odi and amo' and I thought
I really thought it was going to change my life
Be the start of this fantastic new life
And then it just sort of felt like like like
I've felt more satisfaction cleaning my ear with one of
Those stick things
With the cotton on top
That's the God's truth
It felt like a big nothing
Just a thing going into your body
And coming back out again

Blah blah blah big whoop
At least cleaning your ears accomplishes something

Ha okay then

I thought it would change me but I remember
The next day I looked in the mirror
I looked exactly the same
I walked down the street
And I looked at all the grown-ups
And they all looked so boring and blah and
I thought well
It's nothing special
I'm not part of some special club
I'm just the same

Maybe you weren't doing it right

No
I think I was

Or maybe it's not true
What they say about the Italians

It wasn't with the Italian

Whoa
How many boys have you

Never mind
None of your
He's not a boy anyway
He's married
A married man actually
So
I think he oughta know what he's doing

Oh
How long did it last

Each time?
Fifteen minutes or so
We'd just stay in the car

I meant the whole thing

Just for about a year
The school year I mean
He told me we'd run away together
I believed it of course like a dummy

Did you want to

I don't know

Anyway it wasn't true
He had a wife and everything
And in the end he had to cut it off because
My dad's in his department at school

He's a teacher

Mr Shirley

Oh

My Latin teacher
It was a lot of fun I mean really he was
He was a real romantic with the poetry and you know
He used to call me his pearl
You have to open me up to see what's inside
And then
After it was all over
He bought me a pair of pearl earrings
Tiny beautiful pearls
It was all pretty fancy

You ever tell anyone

Who would I tell

I don't know

I'm not the type to sit around bumping gums with
A bunch of dumb girls in the cafeteria

I know
But friends

Sometimes I think I have friends
But then something happens and I realise
I don't have anybody to call

Yeah

There was this one girl at my school
Mary Bruckner
And she had dark hair and pale skin
And then she went away for the summer
She went to camp
And she came back with light hair and dark skin
Her hair had been lightened by the sun
And her skin had been tanned
And so she looked like an exact photographic negative of
herself
She had reversed
Nobody at school could take their eyes off her
And I think that's what I want
I want everything to be the opposite of everything

> *A moment of quiet.*
> > *They listen.*
> > *Gunshots in the distance.*

Hear that?

You mean target practice?
(*With irony.*) For Der Tag
The long-awaited day
When the Commies storm the beaches of Long Island

No listen
I didn't know you could hear it from here

What

Hear the
Maybe it's just in my head

I do
I hear the

No beyond that
If you listen
Beyond the guns
You can hear
Shore birds

> *They both listen.*

I
Wait
Yes

And also

Oh wait I think I do

Do you?

Yes

It's
I think it's

Yes
I do
I hear it

Der Ozean

> *The sound of shooting.*
>> *Is it the ocean?*
>> *Or the sound between gunshots?*

> *End of scene.*

SCENE FIVE

In the woods.
He's doing target practice.

She calls out between gunshots.
Somewhere in between excited
And terrified.

Ich
Ich bin der Jugendredner

What?

Ich bin der Jugendredner
Am I
Am I not pronouncing that
He asked me
Er fragte mich
Er fragte mich

What

He asked / me

Who asked you what

It was totally out of the blue
/ And I'm not supposed to tell anyone
But
Er fragte mich

Wait will you slow down just stop
Wait a minute
Who asked you what
You mean Tommy Lange

Tommy Lange!?
/ No dummy!

Who
Mikey Albrecht

No not that dummy
I don't care about that
That's not even what I'm / talking about

Then what
What are you talking about

Just listen
Listen
Don't point that at me

      He puts down the rifle.
        She catches her breath.

Herr Mueller
He asked me
To be the the
The the Jugendredner

What?!

The youth speaker

I know / what the

At German Day
That's what I'm talking about

That's impossible
It's supposed to be the boy / with the most badges
Is the Youth Leader and the Youth Leader picks the Youth
Speaker

I know I know I know I know I know
I can't believe it I
Ich kann nicht

So what'd you say?

What do you mean what did I say
I said yes
I've never been picked for anything before

Okay

It's never been a girl before

I didn't even know that was possible

It wasn't
It wasn't possible
I said to my aunt this has got to be a mistake
She said no they want you
She said you have worked hardest of any Mädchen or Junge
die Beste Schülerin
And the way I've picked up German and how
I've been perfect
Every test every pop quiz even archery
Aaaah it's sort of overwhelming
Thousands and thousands of people and maybe even the
The the the leader of a whole entire country?!

Yeah I mean yeah
Holy Cow

And I'm supposed to to to
And address them all
Auf Deutsch
I don't even know if I can

Well you don't have to

Well I want to
I do
I have to

Okay

I just
I'm going to
I'm going to pee in my pants

It's
Oh gosh
I think I'm going to throw up

No
Don't

I'm having a a a panic attack

You're okay

My heart is racing
My heart is racing
I can't stop it
I'm going to pass out
I might die
I actually might die right now

> *She starts to hyperventilate.*
> *He grabs her by the shoulders.*
> *Gives her a hard shake or a slap to steady her.*

Hey
You're okay
You're okay

> *She gathers herself.*
> *A moment of quiet.*

I was up all night studying the speeches
Fräulein Hoffer has everything in the library

Okay

Have you read them

You mean from the other German Days

Yes and Hitler

Oh sure

What he says about how change happens
Radical change

'A critical situation cannot be remedied by collaborating with the causes of it'
How can you rely on the custodians of the regime
To change the regime
The parliament the government
That's insane that's impossible
Take things here in America right
We transfer power but nothing changes
Nothing really actually changes
It's all versions of the same thing
Real change requires revolution
But Hitler inherits a country with millions unemployed
A people that has been decimated and vilified by the entire world
And he unites it with discipline and values and hard work and and and he defeats the Communists the Bolsheviks and the chaos
Without shedding a single a drop of blood
Not because he's afraid
This man fought the bloodiest war in human history
But because he knows the cost of violence and and and
You look at what happened in Spain hundreds of thousands slaughtered
And people are giving Germany a hard time how does that make sense

Right well
I don't know about Spain but you know
Usually German Day youth speeches are
More about just camp and fun and hiking and stuff

Don't you care about the world
The politics of it

Of course I do

Are you weak

What?
No

Weak-minded I mean

No I just
I just I mean I don't know all the exact details of it
But I think you can just talk about camp
And camp spirit and fun

Kampfgeist

No
But I just mean regular camp spirit like
Team spirit you know

Uh-huh

Just how much fun you've had
And you know
Everything Fräulein Linda talks about
And community
You for me
Me for you
And sailing

I haven't been sailing

Well we could go

 Pause.

Wouldn't Katie be

That's all over dummy

Oh

You knew that

Well she was blabbing on and on yesterday at lunch

Yeah I bet
She's already with Mikey
She'll probably be knocked up in no time

How's the Italian

There was never any stupid Italian
I mean not really
It was just me
In my mind
And

Oh

I was up all night thinking about it

About what

About the speeches and Hitler
And I could hear marching outside
They were doing
Training drills all last night
I could hear the boots pounding the ground and I felt like
I was just about to jump out of my skin

Yeah I love those drills
And the bugles

And so finally I just I got out of bed and walked outside
and I could
I could see the stars and I thought
Is he looking up at these same stars
This same sky
Like I could almost feel his eyes
These piercing eyes
Bouncing off the sky and back down on me
They can see that far
And then I I I don't know know why I did this but I
Lifted my nightgown up and I pulled it up over my head
And I was
Standing there naked on my aunt's lawn in the dark
And I could feel the breeze on my body and the bugs
circling me
Wanting my flesh
And I thought I could I could just stand here forever and
Let them come for me

Let whoever come for me
I could I could
Feel his eyes on me I could feel him
I just wanted him to come for me
However he wants
And I finally I think I collapsed on the lawn and I didn't
come to until I heard the birds and I ran inside and I

He looks at her.

You're crazy

Help me

With what

My German

Oh

Deutsche Amerikaner or
Amerikanische Deutsche

Uh
Amerikanische Deutsche

Deutsche Amerikaner
Meine Damen und Herren
Volksgemeinschaft
How do you say strong

Stark

Amerika ist Stark

Okay that's good

It is nineteen thirty-eight
We have come through
The War
The Depression immigrants taking our jobs
The pain has broken some
The pain has broken some

Der Schmerz hat einige von uns gebrochen
Es lasst uns nicht unterkriegen
It will not break us
The pain the pain will not break us

Oh

> *He reaches in his trousers.*

Es lasst uns nicht unterkriegen
It will not break us
Es lasst uns nicht unterkriegen

No

Wir fürchten uns nicht

> *Now it's clear.*
>> *He's jerking off.*
>> *She continues.*

Oh God

Der Kampfgeist ist stark in uns
Der Kampfgeist ist stark
In uns

Ohhhh God oh God ohhhh

> *He comes.*
>> *They stare at each other.*
>
> *End of scene.*

The raft in the camp lake.

Moonlight.
    Stars.

They are both standing on it.
    Drenched, in their underwear.

They scream a few times, laughing.

GOD

GOD

HELLO GOD!

GOD!!!!!!!!

        She yells at the top of her lungs:

SAVE US!
FROM HELL!

That's what you want to say to him?

It's just a start
SAVE US FROM HELL
I don't know
What do you normally

WHAT IS YOUR FAVOURITE ICE CREAM FLAVOUR

You're betrunken

No the night air it sobers me up
I'm stone cold

He screams a few more times.

It's fantastic
Nobody can hear you out here
You can scream as loud as you want

> *He screams some more.*
> *Then stumbles.*

Shit
Excuse my French

> *She laughs, then screams at him like a soldier.*

Only German
Only German is sprechen here with Herr Gott

Ja mein Kommandant

> *He falls to his knees.*

Oh look
Ohhhhhhh

What

A
A swan
She's alseep
Look how she tucks her neck in
Ohhhhh
Cygnus
I don't know how to say swan in German

Schwan

Schwan?!?
Really?????

> *She falls over laughing.*

Is that funny?

Schwan!
Are you serious?!

Is that funny?

Schwan it's perfect
It's perfect

> *She calms down.*
> > *Stares up at the stars.*

Orpheus was transformed into a schwan of schtars
And there he is next to his lyre
Lyra
See it?
Cygnus
Lyra
I'd like
When I die
To be transformed into a swan of stars
I want to be
Something less human
And more beautiful

When I die
I want to be like a
Like a
A chicken picked clean

Eeeew

What I mean is
What I mean is
Like I've used every part of myself
And I'm just bones
Chewed clean bones with with
All the meat is picked off
I want to be just plain and clean and
Fully digested and all the way bare
I don't want to leave anything left

I know how you feel

You do

Fräulein Schmidt says I should do a ruthless self-appraisal
A good look or
Like an X-ray or something of of of everything I am
And then I imagine tweezing out all the bits I don't like
Like a
Like a splinter or something and
It hurts yes but I can
I can make myself
Totally clean and then I feel ready

Ready for what

Anything
Der Tag
The day when
If
We have to go to War
Or I don't know ready to get married or have a family or
I don't know what's coming none of us does

You could be a German teacher

A teacher

Not that they still do German in the schools
But they'll start that up again I bet
And I could make furniture
I'm good with my hands

Like our parents ugh
I don't want to turn into our parents

Did you hear that God
Don't turn us into our parents

I mean your dad's a drunk

Fine I know

And my dad's always lost in a stupid newspaper
Shuffling around in his slippers
And I think he probably knew about Mr Shirley

And I think he probably was too weak
To do anything about it

Oh

God I hate weakness I do

One time I went after my dad with a baseball bat

No
You did?!

Yeah
He was beating up on my mom

Really oh my gosh I'm

She was screaming and crying and all curled up in the
corner
And he was standing over her just punching and punching
her
And I went into my room and I found my you know my
Spalding bat
And I came up behind him
He couldn't hear me because he was shouting so loud
And she was crying and the baby was crying too
And I held up the bat
I could have bashed his head right in but she looked up and
saw me
And she said
Stop
And I could tell she was talking not to him but to me
And I could tell right then that
Worse than him beating up on her was seeing me doing it
too

And did he stop
Your dad

Sure yeah for the night

So that's good

It's not good
It's not good dummy
That's what I'm trying to say

What are you trying to say

It's like in wrestling
You know with the Jugendschaft
The wrestling matches and we can win badges and

Yeah

And sometimes I think I'm going to take the other guy's
head and
Just I won't be able to stop
Last week
I did
For a minute
Longer really like a whole ten minutes or something

What did you

I was wrestling this
Well it was
You know James

With the hair

Yes strong kid with that face

Wiry

Yeah

Freckles

Yeah

I know him
He took Emily Fisher into the woods and well
She didn't like what he was doing at all
And he wouldn't even stop it
Nobody listens to the girls here at all

Well yeah well yeah
He's an obnoxious kid and kind of a bully and
Anyway
So we were wrestling and I just
I could feel him getting around my feet
And suddenly I felt like I felt like he wasn't a person
So much as a problem to solve
Like a
Like a really annoying bug
Or a gnat that's just flying around your face
You just want to smash it
I mean that's a thing people do every day it feels good

Sure so then you

So I just flipped him
It felt good
I wasn't even outta control exactly I just wanted
To end it

Right

It was like the anger
It had cleared out my mind and there was
This very clear just 'that's enough' and also I wanted to win
I wanted to win the round

Right well that's

And he went down so hard
I heard his skull make this terrible thud
Like a crack
No you've never heard a sound like this
I swear to Christ it was
In a minute it was like the spell was broken and my
stomach just
It fell through the ground on me and my knees went out and
I just thought
I thought oh God oh God oh God
I've killed him

And I mean he was out
He was stone cold out
And his eyes were rolled up in his head
And his mouth was all slack and then it went hard
Like his jaw seized up and I thought
I thought is-that-rigor-mortis-when-does-that-happen
And I could feel in an instant
This armour grow over myself like okay I'm a killer now
And I will be inside this strange shell peering out
For the rest of my life
It was like a thickening
Or maybe more of a more of a hardening
I thought
This is who I am now
A killer

No

I don't even really know how it happened
And now I'll never come back from it

But you
But he was

He was out
Stone cold out
So they dragged him off the field
Like a dumb sack of potatoes and
We were outside it was so hot
I was sweating buckets and I was delirious I think from the heat
And all the beer and I
Could feel it dripping down my neck and they
They took him to Fräulein Betsy
And I just prayed and prayed

Didn't anyone check for a pulse

Nobody said anything
I mean they just dragged him off

And I guess about forty-five minutes later
Like for those forty-five minutes in my head I was a killer
and then
I get word
He woke up
He's fine
I'm a hero
I won the fight and everyone's laughing about it
But I'm not any different than the person who might have
killed him
I was only saved by
I don't know
The angle
The softness of the ground
Nothing I did is any different

Shhhh
You're not a killer

But that's not
That's just luck
That's just the angle of the ground

You don't have to be

No?

Come here

Don't
I'm afraid of
Myself

You're nothing to be afraid of
Shhhh

How do you know

Because
I see you
I see what you are

And?

You're just
Maybe a bit of a

What
A what

Handschuhschneeballwerfer

> *She kisses him.*
> > *Again. And again.*
>
> *End of scene.*

SCENE SEVEN

Lying in the shade.
  A break in the clearing of brush.

They kiss.
  Through the following they kiss and taste each other.

Sun

Mint

Salt

Salty-mint

Tomato paste
A little bit of tin

Flowers

Something bright
Like a lemon
I want to peel you like a fruit

I want to
Peel off your skin and wear it like a bloody cape

I want to carry you over my head like a prize
Like a torch of fire and and and
And show you off to all those other poor suckers
Who have to live their entire lives without
Seeing you naked

I'll collapse on my knees in front of you
Like a tired pilgrim spent half dead begging for mercy

At the steps of
The steps of of of wherever people pilgrimage to

I want to worship your left pinky toe
And people will see me do it and they'll fall in line
And we'll start a
Worldwide religion dedicated to your pinky toe

The whole world in your perfect earlobe

Your belly button
The whole world in your belly button
I could stare at it forever
Is that navel gazing
I could gaze at your navel forever

Do you think this is the most perfect summer

I know it is
Perfect

Nineteen thirty-eight
I think this is the most perfect
Anybody's ever been together
Is that official or

Probably
Yes
Me for you
You for me

    They kiss again.

Trees

In winter or summer

Spring
That green gold light through new leaves

Maienschein

May-shine yes
There's of course

There's a word for everything in German
May-shine
With a very light breeze
On a hill overlooking a small clear pond
With exactly eighty-six fish

The forest floor
On a very cold day
Sparkling cold
Just after a snow
Layers of pine and crunchy snow and frozen dirt

Banana pudding

Green tea from Japan

The air just before it rains,
Heavy and purple and thick

Babies' hearts

Birds' nests

Blood

> *Pause.*

Do I
Seem different

Is that a trick question

No
Just
Mary Hansen is

You mean

And Sallie Cress
And Martha Rommel and Daisy Lange
Tillie Becker thought she might be
But it turned out to be
Influenza

Are you
Are you

At first I thought I ate something funny
Then I tried a s'more last night I almost threw up

Have you been to see / Fräulein Betsy

Not yet but I know
I missed my / monthly

Oh oh oh oh
Wow

I know

Come here

Careful

Oh no
Did I crush it

No I don't think / it works that way

I'm
(Overcome.) I'm going to be a father

Yes

Oh my gosh this is this is
Wait till I tell my folks
The Runt Triumphant

    He roars.

Silly

This is better than any one of those stupid badges

Well I'd hope so!

This is the
We can have our own life now
We can make our own rules

Wait
Do you love me

Do I love you

Do you
Are you sure

Am I sure
Am I sure
I adore you
I fall at your feet

   He picks her up and places her on the platform stage.

I dedicate myself unconditionally
Unfailingly
Unthinkingly
Unflinchingly
Without a shred of doubt or fear
To you the the the –

God of my Idolatry

Yes

O Romeo Romeo
Warum bist du Romeo

Meine Geliebte
Meine Schöne
My beloved angel
Mein geliebter Engel

   End of scene.

The red flag of the Third Reich drops from the sky. Next to it, the American flag.

The crowd roars.

She stands on the platform.

Takes a breath to speak.
    She cannot.

She takes another breath.

The crowd quiets, waiting for a very uncomfortably long time.

She's gone completely blank.
    She tries to calm herself, grasping for words.

Liebe
Deutsche
Deutsches
Volk

Bundesführer!
Volksgemeinschaft!

Thank you
Danke
Thank you

This is
This is
Wow

What a beautiful day

I love camp
I really I have had a great summer

And I should mention

I built this platform
Brick by brick
Well
I've never done anything like that before

Didn't know
When I built it
That I'd be standing on it myself so
You never know
Things
Do you

>   *She tries to laugh.*

So
Hello

>   *A few people clap at that.*
>   *She grasps for anything to say.*

I love this camp and I love this
Community!

I love all of you
People
I love you
I love you
I love you Aunt Erna

And we have team spirit
That's right
Together we do
We are one people
Stronger together

Tied to Germany
Obligated to America

And that's why we will fight
To rebuild this country brick by brick

If foreign interests
Try to overtake America
We will not let them
We will prevail

> *The crowd roars approval.*
> *She starts to get her footing.*

I am sure
That America can be great again
I am sure
That we the people can come together
I am sure
That our country belongs to the people
I am sure
That our government cannot be trusted to have our best
interests at heart
I am sure
That more senseless war in Europe is not the answer
I am sure
That not another one of our boys shall die on foreign soil
I am sure
That there are spies among us
I am sure
That there is evil among us
I am sure
There are goings-on and all sorts of hocus pocus
Meddlings and those at the very highest levels of
government
Who wish to drag us all back through the muck
Bolsheviks Communists and a global conspiracy of Jews

> *Applause.*
> *Suddenly she's vicious and unafraid.*

We will find them

Die Übeltäter
And tear them out
Rieß sie raus
Tear them out by the roots
Rip them out and tear them to shreds
Grind them into
Staub und Asche
Lock them up and throw away the key
Laugh at them
Laugh at their silly tricks
Lachen ihnen ins Gesicht
When they beg for mercy
Pound them into the dirt under our feet

Nur dann werden wir den Kampf gewinnen!
Gewinne den Kampf!!!!

Nur dann werden wir unser Land zurückgewinnen!

Gott beschütze Amerika and
Gott beschütze das Americanisches Volk!!!

Heil Hitler!!!!

> *The oompah band plays 'God Bless America' by Irving Berlin.*
>
> *She runs off.*
>
> *End of scene.*

Fireworks.

Dark then red.
    Dark then blue.
    Dark then white.

It should feel almost like a
    Coloured strobe
    In very slow motion.

She's standing staring up at them.

He finds her.
    Runs to her.

The following overlaps:

Hey there you are
I was looking all over / for you

I was yeah I know
I was looking / for you too

You musta been flooded with people
Wow you were
That was something

Oh thanks yeah I

That was

Was I
Too much
I don't know because it took / me a moment to

72

No you were
You were great

I was so nervous

Couldn't hardly tell

My legs were shaking underneath me like a leaf
/ I thought I'd blow over

Couldn't tell one bit

My mind went blank
Just a total blank for I don't know how long
I couldn't have told you my own name
It was like everything had gone upside down in my mind
It was like I was naked totally naked and my heart
They say your heart races but mine had stopped
Just stopped dead
And then somehow I started to speak
And I knew exactly what to say and
Everything felt so clear and true and they loved it
They loved me they did
The way they were looking at me all of their eyes on me
All of those people
Forty thousand they said
Forty thousand can that be right

That's right
Forty thousand

All the leaders of the Bund and and and
Herr Kuhn and Herr Mueller

I know

And
Hitler
All the way from Germany

Well no not

What

Oh no just not Hitler

Oh
What

He didn't come

Oh
Really
Are you sure

Yeah
Couldn't you see for yourself

Well there were a lot of people

Yeah but um don't you think he would've stood out

Yeah
I guess

I mean come on

I guess yeah it was kind of a blur I guess

Anyway
What did you think
I mean when you think about it
You really think Hitler's going to show up in Yaphank
/ Eat crabs with us or
Make s'mores

No no no no no no
Right
It's absurd

That was just a thing people were / saying I think

Oh
Sure of course

Just to get us excited

Of course
I'm such a dummy
I mean
I saluted him

So
So does everyone
All the time

Right

I hope you're not disappointed

What
No I'm not
Of course not
Don't be silly
It's just funny that's all
I'm such a dummy
That's all

> *Pause.*
> > *It's tense between them.*
> > *She's unsettled in a way she can't quite understand.*

Wanna go get a s'more

No thanks

Grab another beer
Or ten

No
No I just
I think I just need to sit down / for a second

Oh
Sure
Are you okay

Oh yeah I'm fine
I just need to / sit down is all

75

Here let me
Help you

I'm fine

    She sits.

Can I get you / anything

No I'm just cold
Is it cold

It's August dummy

End of August

Do you think you need the nurse maybe
Is it the

No of course not
I just I'm tired and cold and
I feel like I'm getting eaten alive

You want my jacket
Here take it

No

Oh so now you're mad

Why would I be mad

I don't know
I have no idea

I'm not mad when did I say I

Disappointed
Let down or something

No come on
I'm not

Because of this stupid business / with Hitler

No of course not
I don't care about that
It's just
You know Emily Fisher
She hasn't eaten a bite in two weeks
Ever since she went in the woods with that James
She's wasting away and and and
And none of the grown-ups are saying anything / about it

Well what's that got to do with us

It seems like somebody should
That's all

Look I've been thinking
I'm thinking
About the future

Oh
Sure

Our future I mean

Right well of course

And
I was thinking
Maybe we go out west

Out west?

Nebraska

Oh sure

We don't have to decide now

Right let's not

But obviously we have a lot to plan

Well I know but

I haven't told anyone yet have you

You mean about

The baby
Dummy

No no I

But I'm bursting at the seams

Yeah sure / me too

We're going to want to tell
Our parents and and and
I mean my brothers are going to
Go nuts that the runt got there first
My dumb brother's been dating Polly Gifford all summer
and nichts

Right
Yeah
I just think maybe I just need some time
Maybe to think

Sure of course
One step at a time

         Pause.

How much time would you say
Because it's only nine months away
And that's going to go fast
We'll want to set up a home
Get settled in

Yes of course
It's just a lot to

It doesn't have to be Nebraska

Okay

It could be anywhere Ohio Kentucky

I mean yeah it's just
If it's just uhhh

Because no because
We've been having fun

Yeah
Lots

But it's summer camp
And then the summer's over and

What

Nothing
I don't know
I just need to think or
Maybe or something for a minute that's all

    Pause.

Right

    Pause.

Do you not love me

What

Do you not love me I said

Do you love me

Course I do
I've told you a hundred times

Or was it just the dumb baby policy

What no
What do you think dummy
Why would you even ask me about that

I don't know I'm confused
That's what I'm trying to tell you

You're just scared

I'm not scared

You seem scared

I'm not

Then what

I just think I should just maybe
Go to bed and we can
Talk about it tomorrow

     She gets up to go.

Wait

What

You can't just go like this

It's late
I'm tired

There's dancing

You know I hate dancing

Things are just getting going

No I just
I'm not in the mood

Well you can't just leave like this

I'm just going back to my aunt's

Get a beer with me

No

Come on

No

Well
I'm telling my parents
Tonight

No please don't do that

Why not

Not yet just just just
Give me some time
I haven't even been to a doctor yet

So what

So I need time to think

Think about what

I don't know

(More forcefully.) Think about what

I don't know I said
Anything
Nothing just a minute to
Think for myself
What's wrong with that

Where are you going

I need to go
I don't know
I can't breathe

No
I don't like that
I don't like the sound of that / at all

Well I don't care what you like
I don't care
I'm not yours you know
I don't belong / to you

Just sit down for a minute

No

Sit back down I said

And I said no
Let go of me
Get off me ouch stop

Let go of my arm that hurts
I'll do what I want

You know why you got picked right
For your stupid speech
Because your aunt is fucking Herr Schmidt

No

He's Herr Mueller's brother-in-law
So don't just don't just don't
Don't get too high on yourself

Oh God
That's not true
Why did you ever come up to me

It was pity
You were a scared little dummy
You still are
You're still just the same as the day
I first saw you a sad little wallflower at the dance
/ I pity you

No
That's not true
I'm not afraid of you or of anything
I'll tear this thing out of my body myself –
Rip it out at the root –

> *He hits her.*
> > *She goes down.*
> > *He stares at what he's done.*
> > *Horrified.*

I hate you
I hate you so much I do
I hate you I hate you

Oh God
Oh God

He runs away.
  She writhes in pain.

More fireworks.

End of scene.

SCENE TEN

The ocean.

He sits on the beach, alone.
  Staring out.

Listening to the sound of the waves.
  Looking east.

After a moment, she walks up behind.
  She's shivering a little.

She's not in her camp uniform any more.
  A wool coat is wrapped around her.
  It's almost autumn.

He senses her presence.
  Looks at her.
  Then looks down, ashamed.

A whole summer on Long Island
I never went to the ocean

Yeah well
It's
It's here

What's all that in the water

Leaflets
Pilot missed the camp
Ends up dumping 'em all in the water
Idiots

What do they say

84

He shrugs.
  Looks down.
  Pause.

I came to look for you
This morning
At the Jugendschaft

I was out all night
Breaking down tents

Yes I

You just have to break them down
And roll them real tight
You know for the trucks
Otherwise they take up too much space

Right sure

I just needed a minute to / rest

Look at your hands

Yeah that's just from the rope

They're

That's from the rope
Tying the knots
It's just where I got a callus split open

It looks infected

It's fine
Don't come too close

Okay

  Pause.

I went by your aunt's house
I wanted
I tried to have her tell you I

85

She said / you came by

Then all day yesterday
Nobody even knew where you were
I figured maybe you'd gone back to Baltimore
I figured you hated me
You be right to hate me forever

I just
I actually
I
Went to New York

Oh

Just for the day
So I could just get some time to think things through

Sure that's good
I guess

I took the earliest train
The Siegfried Special
It's not even far

Yeah I know
So
You thought things through
What did you

Well you know
New York's really extraordinary isn't it
It's a lot bigger than Baltimore

Yes

I wound up at the the the
Pennsylvania Station
Which is funny because
Why is there a Pennsylvania Station in the middle of New
York
For a moment I thought oh I've gone too far

Am I in Pennsylvania
But then I realised
No
It's just the way the world is
Nothing makes any sense

Right
So then you were at the station

Right yes and you know I wanted –
I don't really know what I wanted

To think

Yes so I just
I just started walking
That's all I knew to do
I went north

Uptown

I walked through that big park they have there

Central Park

Yes it was all kinds of people
Playing and walking their dogs and eating sandwiches and
I wasn't even sure what I was looking for
I had that feeling
That feeling I get where I want to call someone
But I / don't have anybody to call

Yeah well yeah

So I went to
I found a hotel just off the park
Something fancy and French
And I
Went inside and I found a
A telephone booth

A telephone booth
What for

I didn't know
I just sat there paging through the telephone book
Looking at all the names
And I thought about how it just looks like a collection of
letters
But really each one of those people is a whole universe
And then I
I suddenly realised my feet were hurting like mad

You mean from the walking

And also you know I've got all these blisters and a rash on
my legs
And also you know I've lost three toenails and
One of my toes is just swollen I'm not sure why
So I thought maybe I should see a doctor

So you

My eyes found a a a
Doctor's office

You just found some dumb doctor / out of the phone book

Just wait please
That doctor wasn't available on such short notice
So I kept calling and I called and called
A bunch of them
Until I found someone who could see me right away
It was a doctor
It was a doctor for female things actually
The only one I could find

Oh

So I made the appointment

Oh

And then course as soon as I hung up the phone
I realised
I didn't have any money

It was ridiculous
I couldn't go see some stranger
Some doctor
I didn't have more than enough for a train ticket back and a
Sandwich for lunch
And by the way I was starving
So I figured well that's that I'll just forget all about it

Good

But then I remembered
I was wearing the pearl earrings
From Mr Shirley

Right

I'd put them on to go to the city because
I thought they'd make me look more grown-up
So nobody would bother me on the train or anything so I
I asked the hotel concierge to direct me to a pawn shop
He thought it was funny I suppose people in fancy hotels
Don't pawn things but anyway
I got to the shop and I
I gave them to the man
I thought they were probably just plastic
But he said
No they're real
These are very good-quality pearls
And I thought
Well what do you know
Maybe Mr Shirley did care for me after all

So you got the money

Yes
I sold them to the man
And now I had a fat pocket of money now and I felt good
Because I knew that Mr Shirley did care
And I was also glad to be rid of him somehow
So I I I

So you got to the doctor

Yes I walked in and I was terrified
I was
I almost ran screaming
But his office was very clean and brightly lit and
His wife was the receptionist actually and
I told her
Well I didn't mean to but I told her my whole situation
About the camp and German Day and Der Tag and the
Baby Policy and
My aunt and the stupid girls in the cafeteria
And even about Mr Shirley and everything
And suddenly I was crying and I'm not even sure why
But anyway she gave me a tissue and she said her husband
would help
And I was so scared because
I was worried he could be some kind of a creep
Like Herr Weber or that freckled James
But
He wasn't
He wasn't like that
He was very kind
And he examined me and he said
Well this part is a little embarrassing

What

Because he said
I wasn't
It wasn't
In fact my monthly had come
That very day

Oh
You mean

Which I didn't even
I hadn't even realised it or seen it on my underwear

But I thought

He said maybe a girl can be late due to
The stress of
The midnight hikes or the work
Not sleeping too that can be
Or maybe I was
But then it didn't stick
It was so early

Or
It's my fault
What I did

We can't really know is the thing

It's my fault

He said sometimes a girl can make herself think she is
For months
Even months and months
In her mind
And her body believes it
He said we can make ourselves believe almost anything
He said the best and the worst of us
Is our infinite capacity for delusion

> *Pause.*
> *He's too devastated to speak.*

And then he
The doctor I mean
He took a look at my blisters
And he
Wrapped up my toes in gauze and
That made me cry even more for some reason
And so he said
You need to eat something
Because I hadn't eaten a thing and it was suddenly late and
And so his wife
She was the receptionist

You said

She took me back to their home
Can you imagine the doctor's own home
An apartment really
You had to walk up a hundred stairs and when I got in it
was sort of a mess because the children were running
around everywhere
Two of the sweetest children maybe six and eight years old
Total cut-ups really, Rachel was the older and then little
Sam
And there were coloured lamps with those little tasselled
lampshades and
Books and games everywhere and
Thick soft rugs and little dishes of wrapped candy all
around
And candy wrappers stuffed in the sofa from where Sam
was always
Sneaking candy and the doctor's wife
She didn't ask me anything about anything
She just warmed up some soup on the stove
And fed me and then I was so tired
So tired I could barely move so she put me to bed
In their spare room which was clean and smelled like clean
laundry
And I slept all night

You

And in the morning she had washed my clothes
They were fresh and folded on a chair by the door
And I took a hot shower and then
I ate breakfast with the whole family
The kids are cut-ups we were laughing
And they were so friendly and kind
I don't know if in my whole life
Anybody's ever been that kind to me

    Pause.

And I thought
Oh maybe
This is love
Maybe
This is what love really looks like

So you're saying
Us
It wasn't anything

It's more than just us it's
This whole place
Me for you you for me
The community the kampfgeist
I wanted it all to be true I did

It was true for me

But

I wasn't just pretending
I wasn't just playing little soldier all summer

I know but

I'm going to Germany

What
When

In September

You mean

Well it's almost September now I guess

But when did you

Herr Kuhn and Herr Mueller are taking some of the boys
The best ones
There's a big youth movement over there

Right I know

So a bunch of us are going to join up

But you just
This is so out of the blue

I've been thinking about it for months I guess
But I just decided yesterday
I've been doing target practice all summer
What'd you think that was for
What'd you think we were training for

But what about going west

Some other time

Like when

Anyway west
East
What's the difference right

There's a big difference dummy
It's the complete opposite

I guess I just wanna go somewhere
Be part of something
Serve the greater cause

What cause

Anyway what's it to you
You'll be all the way back in Baltimore

> *Pause.*

Don't go

What

Don't be some kind of stupid German Siegfried
Duped by the gods
Stabbed in the back

94

I'm not
I'm not a hero
I'm not a dupe

What then

I'm a killer I told you
I told you that all along
You were the dummy to believe
I could ever be anything else

But I thought you loved

What

America

I do dummy
I love it so much
I can't stand to watch it all fall apart
Look at this place
Herr Mueller's got FBI all over him
Who knows how long this camp will even exist

Maybe that's a good thing

It doesn't make any difference
They can run us out of town
Rename the streets lock us all up
We'll never stop fighting for what's right
You can't get rid of us
We'll always come back
We'll always be here

You mean
Where

Well
I'll be just over there

What do you mean

95

Well that's the Atlantic right

> *He points straight ahead.*

Yes
Obviously
But it's far

It's not far
It's just right over there

> *The waves are louder.*

Right but

Right out there

Well sure but not

Squint and you'll see me

That's too far to

No I mean it
Try it

It's too far to see

Come on

Now

Yeah
You can do it

Okay
I'm squinting
This is silly

Okay
So
What do you see

I see water
Endless water
And waves and birds

No you have to look farther out

Boats
An oil tanker
Is that what that is

Can you see Europe yet

No

Look harder
Look

     She does.

Oh wait what is

See
See that

Okay
I can almost

See

I can almost see it

Can you see as far as September

Yes
Well but that's not far
It's right around the

Can you see October

You're still there

November

Sure
Yes you're still there

If you look far enough
You'll see the rest of nineteen thirty-eight
Thirty-nine
Nineteen forty

Oh God that all sounds so far away
God Nineteen Forty

I know but look

So futuristic

The future

Look at it

Look

It's so bright

> *They squint into the distance.*
> *Over the water.*
> *As far as the eye can see.*
>
> *End of play.*